Dimples the Snowman

Written and Illustrated by Leona Palski

Edited by Jackie Schultze

Dimples the Snowman

Written and Illustrated by Leona Palski

© 2013 Leona Palski

All rights reserved

11/01/13

Dimples the Snowman

This book is dedicated to my granddaughter Josie

With special thanks to....

Dan
Jim
Bill
Tina

In a cold, but magical place, lives Dimples the snowman!
Dimples has lots of bird and animal friends. Most of his friends live in the woods or on the farm nearby.

His best friend is Little Red, a cardinal.

Every morning Dimples likes to put out birdseed for Little Red and his bird friends.

One cold morning Dimples decided
to build a birdhouse for Little Red.
It made Little Red sing and sing.
That made Dimples happy!

Dimples made friends with the puppy who lives on the farm.

Dimples pats him on the head and gives him a treat.

Now the puppy, named Rascal, comes to see him every day.

Today Dimples decides to spend the day
at the farm.

He sees the pony first.
Dimples offers him a carrot.

Dimples goes into the barn
and in the first stall he sees a mamma cow
checking on her calf.

From the next stall
he hears "naaa".

Two little goats are playing in the straw.

In the
next
stall are
some
pigs
eating their breakfast.

One little pig is in a corner all by himself.
Dimples gives him an apple.

It is warm inside the barn so
Dimples decides to go outside.

On the way out Rascal stops to say hello
to two little donkeys.

The rest of the day Dimples spends with some lively barn cats,

visits and gives grain to the chickens,

plays "Run from the geese!",

goes skating on an icy pond,

and sledding on a snowy hill.

Soon the sun begins to sink
and it is time for Dimples to
go home.

Dimples waves goodbye to all his
friends and starts for home.

On the way home he stops for a moment
to admire the newly falling snow.

After a long day at the farm,
Dimples goes to sleep,
dreaming of all the fun he had.